Tonight We Sleep
with the Window Open

Tonight We Sleep with the Window Open

Poems and Drawings from Belleisle Bay

Melanie Craig-Hansford

Foreword by
Beth Powning

Chapel Street Editions

Appreciation of Place

Chapel Street Editions exists within the unceded and unsurrendered territories of the Wolastoqiyik, Mi'kmaq, and Peskotomuhkati people. The work we do is born from the stories carried by this land and its inhabitants. The animals, plants, soil, water, and air make this place home for the Indigenous people who belong to this land, for the descendants of those who took this land and made it a belonging, and for those who have since come from away. Chapel Street Editions holds a deep appreciation for our place within this land and the stories it tells. We honour the land's Indigenous caretakers and are grateful for their wisdom and guidance.

Published by
Chapel Street Editions
150 Chapel Street
Woodstock, NB E7M 1H4
www.chapelstreeteditions.com
chapelstreeteditions@gmail.com

ISBN: 978-1-988299-49-5

Library and Archives Canada Cataloguing in Publication

Title: Tonight we sleep with the window open : poems and drawings from Belleisle Bay / Melanie Craig-Hansford ; foreword by Beth Powning.

Names: Craig-Hansford, Melanie, 1962- author, illustrator. | Powning, Beth, 1949- writer of foreword.

Identifiers: Canadiana 20220476020 | ISBN 9781988299495 (softcover)

Classification: LCC PS8605.R3465 T66 2023 | DDC C811/.6—dc23

Book design by Brendan Helmuth

Chapel Street Editions, Ltd. gratefully acknowledges the financial support of the Department of Tourism, Heritage, and Culture, Province of New Brunswick.

For
David, Mitchell, and Sloan

And if the world has ceased to hear you,
Say to the silent earth: I flow.
To the rushing water, speak: I am.

Rainer Maria Rilke
Sonnets to Orpheus, Book II, No. 29
tr. Joanna Macy

Table of Contents

Foreword

In her poem, "Sol Invictus", Melanie Craig-Hansford describes the longest night of the year and writes; "I will build you a mattress of lichen and moss/make you a meal of acorn and cone/wrap you in a quilt made from woollen funeral suits…" In like manner, her beautiful collection of drawings and poetry wraps the reader in place—the Kingston Peninsula adjacent to New Brunswick's Belleisle Bay.

Tonight We Sleep with the Window Open will take its place with my beloved, spine-worn volumes of poetry created by writers who have rendered landscapes with emotional precision— poets of place. There are many, but Melanie's book will rest alongside my favourites: Robert Frost, with Vermont's stone walls, snows and white birches; Seamus Heaney, who evokes the blackberries, briars, and milk cans of his County Derry childhood; Allan Cooper's laundry baskets, cats, and rhubarb— spinning the web of Alma, New Brunswick; Mary Oliver's owls, waiting, on Cape Cod.

Nature is preeminent in these works. Daily images, often unnoticed, passed and *by*-passed—dandelions, an errant feather, gravel beneath our shoes—become startling, silvered, sharpened. The natural world—even when juxtaposed with human perplexities—is seen and celebrated as a piercing presence, in and of itself.

Since a particular landscape creates a particular culture, poetry of place is as much about people as it is about nature. In the north, rubber boots are essential in spring, snowshoes in winter. Woodpiles are stacked in sheds; mittens are made with double twists of yarn. The evolution of such necessities as they bloom, fade, and are abandoned over generations imbues the present with a sense of poignancy. This is the interplay of past and present, memory residing in place. The poetry of place is as much about the mundane history of fence posts and teapots, wallpaper and bedsteads, as it is about stars and owls.

Knowing that she will encounter layers of memory in this landscape, even braced for it, Melanie Craig-Hansford returns to Belleisle Bay, the place of her childhood, the hills in which she once felt enfolded. We accompany her on a journey of hope and healing, and participate in a return to ancestral lands.

Tonight We Sleep with the Window Open is divided into two sections: "Footsteps of Home and Contours of Place" describes country life as winter stills the land; in the second section, "The Presence of the Past and Other Voices", we meet the people of the poet's memory. Beautifully choreographed with accompanying illustrations, the whole work is a deliberate and measured examination of a remembered place as it unfolds. "…this home/slow/as awaited spring/sparse as stone."

This place of beauty leads to images of "sea-feathered light, radiance, and iridescent" but often to an encounter with natural predation as well. Many words ring with the shock of this truth—"wound, dead, bleed, clotted, blood, famine".

Her memories move from the realm of dream to the clarity of the real. She sees the placement of constellations as in childhood, smells salt in fog; finds the prints of bedded deer amidst fiddleheads and lady slippers, feels known—even greeted. "This place remembers me/ it rings out with belonging."

In Part II, "The Presence of the Past and Other Voices", people long gone emerge in memory. The dead, Melanie realizes, are imbedded in place even when vanished; they drift on morning light. And we meet them: a mother undergoing cancer treatment; a ghost that haunts an aunt's house; a grandfather with a bucket of berries; a father near death.

The poet visits an abandoned homestead, stands amidst wild raspberries holding a shard of pottery. Within the landscape's memories we encounter the art of hanging laundry, the texture of hooked rugs on bare feet, the laughter of children.

Tonight We Sleep with the Window Open is reverberant with human desire, sometimes passionate, sometimes painful. But perhaps because Melanie Craig-Hansford is a visual artist as well as a poet, she always comes to her work with gratitude and respect for the light of stillness that "bounces/from leaf to leaf/ burnishes bole/ with flashes of stars."

At one point, the play of images creates a movement in which the artist loses and, at the same time, finds herself; "I was sea, a milkweed pod on the cusp/wisps of fallen cloud spores/a wave in an eddy of indigo;/I was light."

With its rich display of visual and verbal images, *Tonight We Sleep with the Window Open* invites the reader to share her journey of hope and healing.

Beth Powning
Markhamville, New Brunswick

Beth Powning is the author of three memoirs, *Home*, *Shadow Child*, and *Edge Seasons*, as well as four novels, including *A Measure of Light* and *The Sister's Tale*.

A Note on Names

The geography of this book is set in the watershed of a great river that the Indigenous people of the region have always called Wolastoq.

French explorer, Champlain, named it the St. John River. At the request of the Wolastoqiyik, a movement is now underway to restore the original name, which this book honours. The first use of Wolastoq is followed by St. John River in parenthesis. Wolastoq is used thereafter.

Preface

The landscape of Southern New Brunswick whispered my name. It is my birthplace. I did not know why I needed to come here, why it was calling me or what I would find when I arrived. I listened and on July 3, 2014, after twenty-seven years of teaching high school in Alberta and Ontario, I arrived for good. I was physically ill, exhausted, and depleted from working full time teaching, raising two boys, and buying into the idea that I could have everything society told me I needed to be happy. This way of living was not without consequence. Ignoring the call to a contemplative, creative life left my spirit broken.

The wonderful teenagers I taught every day did not break me and neither did many of my wonderful caring colleagues...but the politics, the decision makers, the male oriented culture, the emphasis on competition, a bias in favour of a science and math curriculum over the arts did.

Swedish artist and healer, Emma Kunz, said that everything you need to heal yourself you can find within one hundred kilometres from the place of your birth. I was born at the Saint John General Hospital on September 20, 1962. My husband and I had a house built in Erbs Cove, on Belleisle Bay in southern New Brunswick—a tidal arm of the Wolastoq (St. John River) watershed just above Long Reach where the great river slides majestically along the Kingston Peninsula toward the Bay of Fundy. I spent many summers here as a child. It was the last place I felt my authentic self.

I embarked on an eight-year journey of searching, questioning, and following the signs that would lead me to a place of healing. I watched the animals, fell in love with the trees, the rocks, the Bay of Fundy, the shore, and the tides. I floated on the waters of the Wolastoq, I walked hundreds of kilometres in the woods, meditated, learned energy medicine, painted, wrote poetry, got involved in the arts community, met artists and writers, found my tribe.

In 2020 we moved from Erbs Cove to the nearby village of Hampton. The isolation, hard winters, and spring floods were difficult, so we decided to move closer to amenities.

It is now 2022. We are living through a global pandemic, brutal wars rage, and the climate crisis bears down on us. Nothing will ever be the same. But through it all I will be forever grateful to the landscape and people of New Brunswick and all the things I have learned in their embrace. This book is a record of that journey.

Melanie Craig-Hansford
Hampton, New Brunswick

First Acknowledgement

It would be wrong to create a book of poetry about
my love of this province, its landscape and its rivers,
without acknowledging that the lands on which New
Brunswick is situated are the unceded and unsurrendered
territories of the Wəlastəkwiyik/Wolastoqiyik (Maliseet),
Peskotomuhkatiyik/Peskotomuhkati (Passamaquoddy)
and Mi'kmaq/Mi'kmaw. The Peace and Friendship
Treaties that were co-developed and signed with the
British Crown in the 18th century are the only treaties
these Indigenous people ever agreed to. The treaties did
not deal with surrendering the right to lands, waters, and
resources. Although routinely ignored by settlers until
recent times, these treaties remain the legal basis for
the ongoing relationship between Canada, the Province
of New Brunswick, and the Indigenous people of the
Maritime Region.

Map

The upper reach of the Kingston Peninsula is flanked by Belleisle
Bay and the Kennebecasis River. The watershed of Belleisle Creek
feeds into Belleisle Bay, which is an arm of the Wolastoq. Erbs Cove,
the epicentre of this book, is located half way down the Bay.

The map to the right is a detail taken from a book published by the
New Brunswick Department of Natural Resources in 1969.

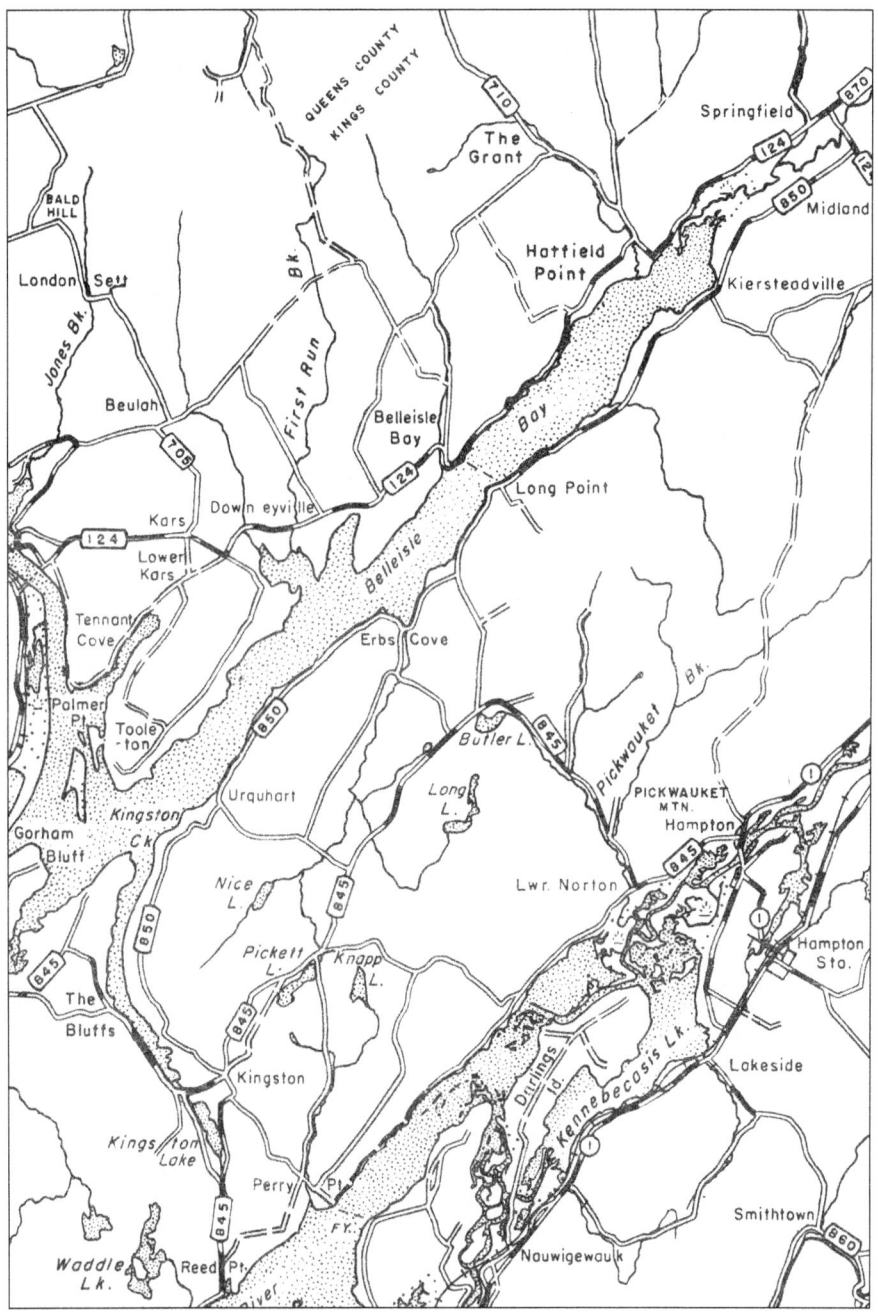

Part I
Footsteps of Home
& Contours of Place

New Brunswick

Called to shore, salt in fog,
follow the tide line and ferry cable.
The lone elm that endured
the Dutch disease remembers
where the dead fell
and the ones that remain
in Nauwigewauk.

My gaze locks constellations
into this place above shivering
tree — sky as in childhood.
Axe handle touched by familiar
hand, bare foot thud
on pine boards, knots
as comforting as memory.
Mother and father rest beneath dust—
painted rock on grave.

Deer tread
over lady slipper and lupine,
purple vetch and strangled daisy:
red in earth   blue in light.

Elements in soil yield mineral
to blood, fiddlehead curls
to loam, June bug beats against
window, marsh fly
through screen,
the sharp smell of cedar.

The pull of moon summons
me home —
this home,
slow
as awaited spring,
sparse as stone.

Whisper

Dream-villains rest
on my pillow,
wait for me to sleep.
Like stars, they appear
from behind clouds.
It's always the same dream—
whispering in my ear to go home.

Erbs Cove—
a place quiet enough to listen.
I say the word silence
like my voice saying the word
doesn't negate its meaning.
As if the silence I long for will emerge
from the mist on the bay.

Out the bedroom window this morning
yellow birch bow to my brokenness.
A donkey-faced deer walks along the ridge
summoning radiance from the woods.
Sunrise breaks through the limbs of trees.
Light fingers embrace me.
I pull my energies in close,
exorcise the toxins
from a life lived fast and loud;
ask the rose light to wash over me.

Mornings in Erbs Cove

There are dreams that reside
with me after I wake:
stories of golden threads
that tether lily pads,
of ferns as tall as redwoods
with moss as thick fog,
of coyotes asleep with me in bed —
cold noses against my cheek —
and snow geese in our field
like mounds of ice,
stubborn against the spring sun,
their wings as wide as dawn.

There are mornings I wake
with impatience on my tongue.
I take my tea outside
to find that sacred time at sunrise
where the chickadees live
and listen for the pause
between the breathings of birch.

There are mornings I wake
to the cedar that genuflects to the rain.
Grey dawn mutes the greening bough,
mullein points to the heavy sky,
drizzle gathers on cricket's back.

There are mornings in Erbs Cove
when winter isolation rings in my ears,
the firewood stack is low,
I've not heard the crunch
of tire or the crow's lament for days.
It's in this first light of stillness
and frost that the birch disappear
against the snow.

If It Had a Sound

winter is coming
my autumn body
must prepare for the cold
raw skin   reluctant
biceps that wane like the moon
breasts as empty as late fall
seed pods
hollow as eagle eggs
before the silent spring
shells as thin as air

brown spots on leaves
brown spots on skin
latitude and longitude lines
trace climate contours
of seasons on sheath

out my window the imbued
stillness of pine
to strip bark
or a word
for *algor*

I have cleared
my garden
of frost
blackened aster and sage

what is winter
emptiness
except a space waiting
to be filled

if it had a sound
it would be the howl
of the tide
between water and ice

I am sedimentary
formed layer upon layer
particles and pith
gravel and snow
pressure like ice against stone

February

I am an ice-fishing hut,
vulnerable, exposed,
a reluctant refuge for the icy wind
searching for a place to rest.

In this snowless February,
melancholy falls like mourning,
blankets the bleak
world in grey.
White hares wake to frost in fields
the colour of umber,
like shellac on old pine.
There is no snow to insulate
next summer's strawberries.
Seeds shiver beneath sunless skies.
Spring moss will remain parched—
brittle beside irrelevant puddles.
Winter will not fulfil its need to quench.
This snowless February is disarmed
like the meagre ice that flows to Fundy
and the sun that has nothing to melt.

Sol Invictus

Today, an evergreen —
I decorate with light
as the sun moves
along the horizon,
its meagre glow falling
behind knit branches.

In the gloaming, I carry a flame
into this darkest of nights
in honour of the famine months,
animals in cave and cavern
birds long turned south,
even the fireflies have spent their quota
of limelight.
Under the frozen bay
blackness,
sturgeon retreat to the bottom
as you tilt away from earth.

On this darkest of nights,
Sol Invictus,
I will weave you a crown of cedar,
build you a mattress of lichen and moss,
make you a meal of acorn and cone,
wrap you in a quilt
made from woollen funeral suits
to hold you alive against the night.
This winter solstice has taken our breath
and written our names in ink
as opaque as the heavens.

On this longest night,
frigid air longs for a scent to hold
but shadow buries its perfume
beneath the soil.
The slate sky carries your grief,
shoulders your pain.

Dark spirits walk with us,
whisper Yule tidings,
offer up a prayer
that city dwellers,
who have never known
the ebony of night,
learn to look at the stars.

For eons, this day's sunset has shone
through lintel and post.
What will become of the stones
if they outlive the light
that set them in place?

Sol Invictus,
this is a different world
than that of the ancestors.
I see you are weary,
your chariot old,
your horses want to relinquish
their reins.

On this darkest of nights,
I pray to you
that obsidian
will not be the colour of dawn.

The Silent Treatment of Ice

A crow picks at new ice
confused by a relationship
with water that is now hard.

Ice moans from one end
of the bay to the other
like the exhale of an angry lover.

A loud crack disturbs
the sturgeon and bass
who,
like me,
escape to the safety of weeds,
mud, and shell—quiet
in our resolve
to outlive the splintered
world above.

The crow follows me. Frozen
shards of rigid frost pickets
trim the shore, slow me down
as I traverse harsh terrain.

Today's cold hardens smells, crawls
under our door and cracked
windowsill. Through the glass,
I see him ignoring the frozen
words that hover between us.

From the cedar that snaps in the stove
I watch what we had go up in smoke.

Patterns on the Periphery

Six spots in the snow
beneath the cover of conifers
tracks lead there   then away
a sequence of scat
dots of yellow
patterns on the periphery
in the muffled silent snow

I push past in the snow
not wanting to disturb
their beds
they may return
in the gloaming
in the muffled silent snow

Six deer asleep in the snow
oh, how I wish I was a bird
watching them breathe
small puffs of white breath
a rhythm of snores
chanting out in the stillness
in the muffled silence of snow

Kneeling in the snow
I put my hand
on one of the circles
feeling for
residual heat
but this morning's chill
has frozen their slushy beds
no scent or heat remains
in the muffled silent snow

How many would notice
the sacredness of this spot
the remnants of a night
spent huddled for warmth
bedding down against the threat
of weather   wolf
coyote   cougar
in the muffled silent snow

No human hunters in the snow
no shots ring out in this season of white
the deer know their safety
is in this circle of generations
the insulation of other whitetail
hiding on our trail
in the muffled silent snow

The Possibility of Light

My house is surrounded by mullein,
tall spikes with yellow flowers,
black spears in winter.
It's my spirit herb.
It will protect me.
I will make a tincture.

Earlier that evening the sun
travelled along the horizon
as the day dropped into darkness.
Now, this night in March
has lost its moon as a storm
comes across the bay.

Mullein seedpods blow outside
my window and in their wildness
point to the heavy sky.
As they sway, they measure
the width of the wind.

There is a place of stillness
to which I go when life turns black.
It first appeared in a sea-feathered light
casting shadows on the trail
along the Bay of Fundy.
In the air's damp breathe of rotting meadow and tide
solid became vapour,
a resonance of viridian—
no path   no fence   no other.
I was sea, a milkweed pod on the cusp,
wisps of fallen cloud spores
a wave in an eddy of indigo;
I was light.
Then everything slid back in line,
the waves crawled into place
and the sky once again spoke of blue.

In this night's darkness
a new appreciation for moonlight.
I face east so I can wake
to the radiance of morning
even in its winter thinness.

This night I will dream
rows of yellow flowers
and of farmers who used dead
spikes for torches.
Now, like so many things,
mullein will hold the possibility
of light.

Starvation Wound

I

Autumn

Today we long for the freshness
of snow as we walk in the rain.
The path to the beach passes
old vertebrae, deer scat, and a dead hare.
The dog rejoices in the decay
and you in breathing autumn air.

Ditches, like veins, bleed water and silt.
Through clotted culverts the fast water slows
around rotted asters and brown leaf wilt.
The bay is edged in feather ice,
open water the colour of slate.
The high tide line marked by debris,
soggy bark, eel grass.

A deer;
all that remains is a pelt
and brittle bones,
ribs like flying buttresses
holding up the firmament.

Our dog, hushed into silence, shakes with excitement.
We watch the feast, entangled wings and growls.
Crow, turkey vulture, and eagle compete,
stature determines place.
An eagle pulls bloody threads of muscle
from exposed ribs,
pink in the gloaming
and flies off when he sees us,
his flap expelling a draft.

Inside, the dog rushes for the water
dish and you to stoke the stove.
The three of us hover around the blaze
and settle into the aroma of fire and frost.

II

Winter

In the blizzard,
snow laden evergreens bend over deer's well-worn path.
Tomorrow they will follow the same trail under the snow.
Tonight, they will dig hollows to wait out the wind,
lay their heads down beneath the snow swollen sky,
wake in the morning as white mounds on the forest floor.

III

Spring

Cedar announces the coming of spring,
a gesture glinting through boughs, umber limb to green.
The grey scale of winter fades.
Waving branches announce the northeast wind.
Time is measured in shallow roots.
Fallen logs remain a testament to frost.

Bucks welcome new antlers.
Scraped velvet clings to sun warmed bark
but this hard winter lingers.
Deer trample mute trails in wet snow.
The world is hungry, the cry of empty bellies
shout from limb and snowpack.
Copulation is postponed.

A doe bends her head and nudges her fawn.
The newborn stays on shore.
She walks out onto the snow-covered ice
and looks to the opposite horizon.
The snow is deep,
one leg goes through, then another.
The journey to the other side of the Bay is difficult.

She trudges forward alone;
the other shore beckons with the promise
of low boughs and exposed lichen
while wind and icy pellets stab her ears.

A noise behind her —
trees rustle,
branches snap,
howls of coyotes,
growls of the pack.
Her fawn will not fight.
She quickens her pace, climbs the opposite bank,
takes safety in shore bush and shaded stone.
Boughs eaten clean and the promise of lichen, dashed.
She is without the advantage of others to scout out exposed
undergrowth, abandoned bird feeders and apple wind falls.
She forges onward along woodlot trails and property lines.

A crow watches the coyotes' feast on the shore
waiting to forage leftovers, spilled intestines.
The plague of hunger also pursues him,
famine has wings.

Deprivation drags onward
like a carcass hauled across the ice
leaving a crimson slash,
a starvation wound
upon the frozen wasteland.

Sea Glass Grows Sharp

On this morning's walk
ice darkens
under storm clouds
as cold as graphite.

Beneath the frozen bay
tides turn to currents
of howling widows.

Waves hit the underside
of ice in brute thugs,
a woodpecker's swoop—
startles.

Imprints of last night's copper
sunset fade like the sound
of your boots next to mine.
The narrative we spoke each
day on our walks is hollow
without you beside me.

The old wooden door that slaps shut,
our symphony of wind chimes—
they change in the hearing
with fewer ears to harbour sound.

Your fingerprints
on beach stones
disappear in dust,
our collection of sea glass
grows sharp.

A Longing to Cling

Fog drapes barren hills,
a dash of gold breaks the horizon,
disrupts the bay's tendency toward sky.
A lone branch in stone encrusted soil
supports a bird whose grateful claws
cling to the yielding wood.

Cedar grips the rocky shore with roots
grasping stone like cold arthritic hands.
Frozen high bush cranberries
cling to branches for birds to strip clean.
An owl lines up limp squirrels
on a bank of traffic darkened snow,
then carries them away in hungry talons.

I cling to the hope
I do not grow accustomed to the cruelty in this place:
ducks frozen in the first layer of winter ice,
deer falling through the last of melting spring ice.
Mutilated raccoons' intestines spilled in crusty ditches,
hunter's trophy carcass strapped across the hood of his half-ton,
roadkill left to melt into piles of bones.

To cling is harder than the invention of stone,
like the old beard moss that drapes naked
branches, mint green against the white winter sky.

This Place Remembers Me

Regrets are stacked
beside the wood pile.
Apologies rent space
in my winter brain.
Today, the snow calls me out to play
but disquiet has kidnapped my limbs.
Lament clings to the straps on my snowshoes.
Today, snow angels have no wings.

And what of the ermine's regret
that the universe could have turned his coat white
after the first snow fall instead of before.
In the spring he will turn back to a brown weasel
as big as the knots in my shoulders
carrying the burden of my repentance.

When you followed me to the bay,
we left behind our shared histories
and silent-centered forests.
This place remembers me,
it rings out with belonging.
This is where larch is named tamarack,
where wet ground and spring nourish wild
parsnip and fiddleheads, where eagles soar
through the lens of your binoculars;
a place that offers a new way of looking
at stars,
the joy of deer in the morning, and
your first real blizzard.

Tonight We Sleep with the Window Open

Open the window,
banish the stale,
welcome the breezes,
gritty
from a dance with the last
blackened snow.

Renew our acquaintance with the opus
of peepers and cadence of loon.
Archive the breakup and the cresting freshet,
the first sign of daffodil.

Air out the woollen blankets and eider down,
the thick smell of lanolin and damp duvet.
Wooden pegs perch like birds on our clothesline,
sagging with the weight of winter bedding.

Smell the leaves rotting on new grass,
the sweet stench of manure,
feces dissolving into new mud,
the metallic scent of recent water
from beneath frozen ground.

Sweep off the porch,
dust off the wind chimes,
banish the remnants of a long winter's fugue,
measure the thin roots that stand
against winter winds and fallen logs.

Tonight, we sleep with the window open,
listen for the long-silenced surf,
the unfurling of fern,
and grasses alive with crawling…

Saint John

The silence beneath the stilled
foghorn is palatable.
Uptown, the talk on the street
turns its face to the sun.

A woman on the bus stares
past me out her window
holding onto the possibility of bicycles —
counting spokes between sighs.

Wind from the bay scatters
garbage and the homeless
on King Street —
Grey stretches of dust and grime scream
to be swept up and replaced
with red and yellow tulips.

Today, it's like explosions
at the refinery and scrap yard
and murder on Canterbury Street
have been momentarily forgotten.

On a hill above Saint John
the ghost of The General sits.
The memory of my parent's first meeting
and my first breath remain on that altered horizon.
Today, even the past is forgiven
by the ones who watched it implode.

On Queen Street a girl in a pink coat sees her shadow.

Flood 2018

Through her window—
the river.

Each spring it rises,
rolling down stone-stained streams,
around ice flows stacked
        randomly on shore.
The snowpack rapidly melts,
        swelling the Wolastoq.

The high water is cold,
        the colour of weak coffee with cream.
It smells of rusted iron hinges,
        the mouldy sneakers of teenage boys.
The trees drink their fill of waters
        full of shit and silt.
The loons have lost their nests,
        their mournful cries confuse the crows.

From her kayak, a skim of fir,
        tamarack needles, hemlock and cedar bough.
She loosens her grip on the paddle
around driftwood bleached
        to a pale shade of sun.
On shore, piles of branches and sticks
like dishevelled nests woven by maniacal birds.

A trailer left unattended
in a once-grassy field,
          now submerged.
Pickerel swim in and out of slider windows.
The water is high enough to float
a bloated deer carcass on a tree branch
          hanging low with unfamiliar weight.

Paddling down washed-out roads,
a beaver swims across her path,
          stick in mouth.
He is re-building his lodge on higher ground.
He does not resist the rise and fall of water
          he knows not of floods.

Water recedes lower than tragedy.
With beep, beep, beep,
the backing-up trucks dump a cascade
          of rocks and sand
filling in sections of eroded road
around dumpsters with washed
          away histories and hysterics.

At the peak,
all she can do is wait.
The patience of the beaver and loon
          remind her of what she has forgotten.
In the stillness of receding water,
          the river swells within her.

Flood 2019

On this morning,
the snowpack up north
is as thick as woollen socks.
The air is too cold for salt.

The water moves south.
Without the resistance
of sandbags, the water will rise.
When the fog lifts, the air
will have ice fingers.

Trees bend to the weight of spring.
A raccoon carcass washes up on shore,
gnawed and gouged by carnivorous teeth.

On this morning,
I dance to the ruckus of scavengers—
submit to the will of water.

Gift of Gills

I am beneath the floodwaters
I look to the sky through liquid
that softens the edge of clouds

forests fall
waves slap swollen ground
so saturated it cannot hold more
water so filthy it cannot satisfy thirst

a bass floats above me
predicts a shift with dead fisheyes
a stone sinks past my face
I look through the rings —
trace the loops
to where certainty disappears

I am back at the beginning
I have gills
I say the earth's ageless names
in honour of what we have squandered
I let go of the things that have grounded me
deny my gift of gills
sink to the murky bottom

Rituals to Prepare for the End of the World

In my studio,
I paint a green stripe
down my nose in honour
of the prophet Matisse,
place sunflowers on my sill,
sing in praise of yellow,
and light a candle in honour
of Mary's geese.

I say a prayer to silence —
find my peace
in the gaps between the seasons,
look to each day for stillness
in the slack time of tide.

An artist planted
hundreds of rhododendrons
at Shamper's Bluff
where Belleisle bay
meets the Wolastoq
and Kingston Creek.

It is there I will wait,
beneath the blossoms
held in the arms
of this sacred place.

Naked

This spring, I wrote my last newspaper column.
My photo and by-line gazing out at the reader
destined to line the bottom of bird cages —
parakeet shit on my face.
Or, along with kindling, my naked expression crumbling
to black, exposed to the elements of feces and fire.

Thinking of bird shit
on my drive to Saint Martin's this morning—
suddenly, sixteen deer on a hill
in a field of thinning snow,
patches of new grass in the undergrowth.

They glance up, undeterred.
No fear flips their tails.
Come fall they will move back into the woods,
defenceless against bullet and arrow,
but for now, they are safe.
Their fur resembles the colour of the ripe
mudding soil as they disappear against the landscape.

Along the road, red osier dogwood flourishes
in ditches still full of snow.
Tongues of fire licking the thin air—scarlet
against the starkness of spring.

I cross the Kennebecasis River
on the bridge at Apohoqui.
The water is low—
rocks usually hidden by a rushing flow
are bare and look to the slim spring sun.

In Saint Martins, the red mud of the Fundy shore
is exposed at low tide—
raw like a third-degree burn,
raw like the winds of April.

In spring we expose ourselves to her ripening,
like the river rocks, salty mud flats, and deer.
And like those reaching ruby branches
of red osier dogwood—
undeterred by their nakedness.

Listening to Billy Collins Read Poetry while Painting on My Deck

Belleisle Bay—
there on my canvas
the view from my deck

the smell of last night's campfire
hovers drone-like
in the air

the bay beyond the trees
intervals between branches
splashes of blue through green

Billy says his dog
has returned from the dead
to tell him he never liked him

suddenly, a cigar boat distracts me
the roar as annoying as a drunk
neighbour asking for a light

for his fireworks—
I bet his dog doesn't like
him either

I see a loon ride the wake
of a jet ski
another boater high

on speed and liquor
as Billy tells me I should
throw myself at the wall of life

oh how I wish that
boater would encounter
a wall

in this place on the Bay
be it by beer or beauty
we have all come to forget

Reflections

for Margie

That night we discussed the importance
of reflection on water and friendships
and of light in windows
like the time you found a pileated woodpecker
on your deck,
feet in the air like a bad joke —
a punch line of feathers plastered to the glass.

And there was time you tried
to capture the blue of the Bay,
its stillness reflecting clouds.
You poured it into a bowl
hoping the image would remain
but it was just clear water after all.
You said at least at dusk there
will be another sunset lighting
up the birch in shades of orange and pink.

You told me the dash of light
along the horizon as the sun disappears
is the lifeline tethering you to this place.
It reminds you of the night we lay
in the grass waiting for the northern lights
that CBC said were sure to appear.

That evening we watched fish jump,
eating flies and slapping sea lice
from under their scales,
hundreds of concentric rings spreading
at intervals on the water
in sync with our breathing,
our laughter bouncing back
from the other side of the Bay.

Ferries of Southern New Brunswick

He is getting too old to sell
his mamma's muffins,
walking the yellow line
at the Gondola Ferry.
He looks in the car windows
for hungry passengers.
No takers today.
He dreams of Alberta
where the work has dried
up but he doesn't care —
the prairies mean freedom.
He plans his escape, dreams of
the day he will get off the ferry
on the other side.

Uncoil me like the ferry's cable.
Let me loose to skip across the bay.
If I were a prairie fence,
I could say everything
there is to say about the grass
on the other side.

She sits on the jumping log,
dangling her feet in the Wolastoq
the water as warm as puddles in the sun.
She watches the Evandale Ferry
and the boats docked at the Hotel's slip.
People getting gas and ice,
laughing and singing and holding
up bottles of beer. She chews
on the end of her braid and wonders
if she will ever be rich
enough to have a big boat
and spend the day on the other side.

I am the ferry captain;
I wait out the storm, the breakup of ice,
the awakening of spring, the congestion of boats.
From the wheelhouse, I can see both sides
of the river, and, like the gull
soaring overhead,
I am grateful for the perspective.

He is parked in line waiting
for the Deer Island Ferry.
Light shines through
rusted holes in his car
like eyes in the ditch at night.
His sweatpants sag, the elastic gone.
His yellow t-shirt transparent
as morning. A trunk full
of periwinkles in mesh bags on ice,
he continues to scavenge while he waits.
He hopes to sell them on the other side.

I am the soil, stone to dust,
star atoms to loam.
Trim the fat, collapse the bones
into the essence of water.
Ferry me to the other side,
surround me with ferns and right whales —
gently place periwinkles in my hair.

Dragonfly

This afternoon on the beach
I hunt for flat rocks—
flatter than the earth before Galileo.
Ash trees cast shadows.
Dragonflies taunt my dog.
He swims back and forth,
tries to catch them in his mouth.
They are like little helicopters,
now with a live soundtrack of war.
Fifty kilometres away
at Gagetown Canadian Forces Base,
training exercises are underway.
Heavy artillery sounds like thunder
on a cloudless summer day.

I thank the dragonflies for exercising my dog.
His attention shifts to eating waterweeds
and discovering the same rock over and over.
His thirst satisfied by lunging headfirst into a wave.
He circles three times, empties his bladder,
then returns to the dragonflies.
He loves the water so much he forgets to stop—
ignores his desire to rest, like a toddler confused
by her exhaustion.

The sun comes around and overpowers
the ash leaves, light falling full on my face.
Oh, could I shake away my restlessness
like the dog shakes water from his crinkly fur
The showering droplets cool me—
heavy artillery keeps me on edge.
The dragonflies don't seem to notice,
wings against the breeze,
hover
give in
float away.

Painting Saint Martins

I gathered smooth stones
as round as a gull's eggs
and hard as last year—
their sharpness
worn clean as glass.

I brought them home,
arranged them in a bowl.
My canvas primed—
ready to accept their image
in shades of sand and sky,
to tell their story
of tumbling and loss,
of yesterday's waves,
and their reason
for being stone.

Tamarack

My dog runs ahead in the forest,
stops along the trail to sniff
and tell his story to the undergrowth.
Sticks and seeds cling to his tail.

An eagle overhead
casts a shadow on moss.
Oh, to learn to trust
this life and our place in it,
like the eagle trusts the strength
of the highest branch on the hemlock.

The tail end of hurricanes
have stripped trees bare.
Tamarack lose their needles last,
golden spires above hills
of grey bark and black evergreens.

The tamarack stands
confident
in its connection to the stars,
feels the energy of the other trees
coursing through the roots
within the soil.

Like my dog,
the tamarack does not question
its place in the forest.

Behind the Veil of Light

I dreamt there were coyotes in the alders,
their tawny eyes beg me to come out and play.
Wood fairies dance; iridescent wings,
ruby ribbons trailing as they twirl
in and out of the gateway between the trees.
The shriek of a crow from above; as she flies over
her shadow slides across
me like a prophecy.
I quiver within
like leaves of aspen shiver in the breeze.

In the dream, strangers walk the beach
in front of my house collecting smooth stones
and sea glass. They place them on my windowsill.

I wake to a red sky,
wonder who these strangers are.
I must prepare for departure.
My ears must gather sounds,
eyes must save images,
memory will assemble sunsets;
leave behind my old self,
the one who would not play with the coyotes
to expose her wild self among the alders.
I will place her fear in a sealed canopic jar
beneath the cedars.
The one who didn't trust in the knowing behind the gauze,
I will put her scepticism in a velvet bag under
the granite boulder beside the beach.
The one who didn't dance with the fairies,
I will bury her trepidation in the soil beneath the lupines.

I have collected all that I was meant to gather
from this place on the Bay.
I have swaddled intuition in solitude,
gathered mysteries from behind the veil of light,
from the rustle of pebbles and from
the cloudless summer sky that now lightens
as it bends shoreward.

Many visions have appeared to me
from beneath the wings of crows,
but on this morning,
cloaked in scarlet
light,
a premonition.

Processing Cedar

I

On the Bay
ice as thin as patience
everything is grey
the ice
the fog
the lichen covered cedar

gulls scream
themselves hoarse
deer paw
their hooves raw
osprey flap
themselves spent

no need to listen
for the news
town criers declare
invisible microbes
have arrived on our soil

a quarantine
seal up your houses
mark your death door
for fear spreads faster
than fleas
add the departed
to the death carts
record their names
on the bill of mortality
dip their coins in vinegar

II

we make masks
turn whiskey stills into vats
of assassin gel
vilify bats

III

isolation
forces me to stay
at the water's edge
each day
like the last

no need to practice
a safe distance
I am the only one
on the shore

the world shifts
the moon has turned red
even the wind has stopped
seeking branches to break

none of us can breathe

on the shore
a cedar
I kneel before her
remove a rock beneath her root
sit in the hollow

chainsaws in the distance
your bark coils inward
you know naught of fear
pain   yes
or I've heard your fallen cries
have watched your broken limbs
succumb to gales

you have captivated me
your lower branches
bleached titanium in the sun
like brittle bones under foot

oh cedar
teach me how to resist
the world's propensity for rot—
how to stop this erosion
how to be still

Evolution

Yesterday, a bird slammed
headfirst into my window;
left her brain matter
and a smear of feathers.

I know birds were here long
before windows,
but you stupid bird,
haven't you evolved
enough to understand reflection —

haven't we?

November

Cold rain
on blueberry fields
of burnt sienna,
rusty turf,
golden straw,
neon mounds of lichen.
In the diffused afternoon light
I am captivated
by colours that shimmer
with such a force.

Outside the car window
the same view,
but you do not see what I see.
I am overwhelmed
by the sacredness of what
my eyes can hold.

Light changes by the season's arc of the sun.
Fields along the Bay of Fundy
cling to small scrubby evergreens,
bare garnet dogwood—
even the granite boulders glisten
pink beneath a layer of water
on feldspar and quartz.

Time

There are erratics
behind my house,
giant stones scattered
by the gradual retreat
of glaciers.

Slow, like the symbiotic
gathering of algae and fungus
where sea meets land.

Slow as lichen that crushes stone.

Slow wants to find me now
but life seems to retreat
faster than it used to.

If only glaciers
could teach me how
to live
one centimetre at a time.

Still Life with Partridge

A partridge slams
into our window,
breaks her neck.
So close I can see the
brown and white mottled feathers
of the chest rise
into her last breath.

From the window it is
like looking at a painting
by an old Dutch master.
Always a still life
with a wild feathered
beast,
broken necks limp
on gathered cloth,
red spittle like crushed raspberries
on blue-green satin,
along with a half-peeled lemon
so yellow your mouth
salivates in anticipation
of its sour burst.
The olives shine out loud
with their version of green.
You know that wine
will live up to its colour,
a maroon so deep it's
almost black, gift of
the Italian sun and
days of fermentation.
A silver chalice
reflects the colour
of death and the broken
necks of a medieval feast.

Pleated Out of Existence

Beneath my scarlet umbrella
yellow begonias turn the colour of salmon.
This is the underbelly of the lost
hours spent on my deck.
Today, my world struggles to be rosy
as my geraniums gather in praise of red.

My shed is full of tools
I can no longer use —
how hard it was to give up
digging
raking
planting.

My garden succumbs to weeds
and the repetition of perennials,
the hill covered in scented geraniums,
buttercups in ditches,
lupines gone to seed —
those little furry seed pods
like the underbelly
of the dragonfly
that lands on my shoulder to rest.

tell me about your travels, little one —
your ancestors
your darkness

This morning when I opened
my scarlet umbrella
there was a moth caught in the folds —
pleated out of existence
until I let it go free.
Today, I feel
pleated out of existence,
tired…
not the person you see
but the part that animates me.

Morning in the Studio

Crows on bare branches—
a racket of corvid blather
about the murder down the road.
They answer each other in sequence,
allowing space between messages.

Missed opportunities—
rabbit road-kill   squirrel in ditch.
A banquet laid out in potholes,
an early spring repast.

The March sun is thin,
the ground confused
by a cycle of
freezing and thawing.

My limbs are heavy
like movement through paint.
I want to make marks
like the scratches of claws.
I channel stillness
to the rhythm of caws
at my studio door.
I listen for the dialect of birds.

Paths on stretched canvas—
trails to nowhere.
I dream solid into sand,
rip jagged lines,
tear at the paint,
puncture lesions on gesso—
gashes like bone on bone.

Shapes emerge from beneath
layers of milky mist.
From the staccato of feathers
a cacophony of sinuous smears—
a record of my morning slowly appears.

Reaches of Sound

A Northern Flicker
taps on my chimney cap.
He declares
the size of his territory,
defends the reaches of sound.
He measures his past and future
by the time it takes
to fly over his domain.

My morning tea holds
the ripples of his raps.
His cries,
now far off and hollow,
wail on the wind.

I sit in isolation in the slender
spring sun
beside the woodpile sheltered
from the cool April wind—
read stories of my ancestors.

My dog collects rocks,
seemingly frantic they will
one day be gone.
He buries them with his bones
in the soil of our yard.
He measures time
by the depth of his relics.

I feel old
and my expectations have dwindled —
no longer expansive
like the forethought of youth.
This is the way it should
have been from the start.
It was always an uncertain path,
as unpredictable as spring floods
and viruses
that hitch rides on world travellers
who think their prospects
are as big as oceans.

I hold my uncertain fate
with soggy tissues.
I take them
from my pocket and tuck
them in the sleeve of my cardigan
like my grandmother.
I look to her memory to learn
the secret of survival.

I clench my teeth,
draw lips
into a thin line of resolve,
let out a sigh.
On this cool spring morning
of flickers and dogs
old age has found me.
Like the earth,
our future has diminished
to the reaches of sound.

Part II
The Presence of the Past
& Other Voices

As If We Have All the Time in the World

My mother's caftan
was blue and green paisley
with peacock feathers and emerald leaves
blowing against azure sky.
She would put it on at the end of the day
when she changed out of her slacks.
She would take off her girdle, bra and prosthesis,
hand her fake breast to whoever was standing nearby
asking the unsuspecting visitor to feel
how life-like it was. "Silicone, like a real boob," she would say.

That winter of chemo, Gravol, and pocket novels,
she would spend her days lying on the couch.
My sister and I would come home from school for lunch,
eat Kraft dinner, and watch *The Price is Right*.
She would ask us to stay home for the afternoon
to watch the soap operas with her. We would laugh
and say how funny it was that a mother
would beg her children to play hooky from school.
As if we had all the time in the world
to watch *The Edge of Night* with our mother
as if she would be on that couch forever.

Those first days of March
the sun came around the side of the house
to shrink the piles of old snow.
With sun on our faces, the promise
of skipping ropes, hopscotch, and
warmer weather, summer
stretched ahead forever.

Years later, I met you.
You made me laugh like my mother used to.
I read your palm, made sure your lifeline was solid and strong.
Under the sunset over Lottie Lake, I knew you were the one
with whom I could create a new possibility of forever.

Today as we walk along Belleisle Bay
I feel that same promise of warmth
from the March sun on my face,
smile as it highlights your hair and beard,
now grey. Reflecting on our many years together,
forever feels a lot closer now.

A Reason for Being Stone (A Sestina)

my mother and father lie still in silence
eyes rest on lath and lichen
clapboard white; in the yard a church
eaves stuccoed with the nests of swallows
time measured in moss on stone
three windows long, two wide   stained glass

viridian light from the panes of glass
my mother and father lie still in silence
today their breath softens to stone
faces mint, the colour of lichen
lofty prayers, the swoop of swallow
in the clearing that circles church

hymns ring out from the small white church
on the altar communion wine   a single glass
above the pews   offspring of swallow
my mother and father lie still in silence
fingers grasping at wings of lichen
the smell of pine needles and stone

they know the reasons for being stone
ancient ones   the bedrock of church
from the basement the song of lichen
echoed by the shattering of glass
my mother and father lie still in silence
sinew and sweat the builders of church
to God a liturgy of lichen

soil crusted with torn lichen
hollow bones of kin and swallow
wind through pine   chimes of glass
a walkway   a puzzle of stone
it leads to a gate closed to the church
where my mother and father lie still in silence

in the church yard   a granite stone
shadow cast by a small white church
my mother and father lie still in silence

Bitter Bleach and Brine

for Gig and Snooks

She lingers on the landing,
unravels carpet cord to trip us,
waits for us to climb the stairs
then sits on the edge of the tub,
watches us pee.

My sister smells her close
like pickle juice and Comet cleanser.
I say she smells of bitter bleach and brine.

She watches when we venture
to the attic where the train sets,
rusty toy tanks, and Chinese checkers live.
She hides among the combat-worn uniforms
that hang in a row. The buttons and medals
rattle in her breeze.

She wears Aunt Dolly's red lipstick,
uses Dolly's brush to remove tangles
from her copper-coloured hair,
leaves behind a strand to remind
my aunt she is still there.
If we sleep in her bed, she hides
our stuffed animals. If we leave
our baby-powder footprints
over hers
she makes our eyes water with her stench
like rotten eggs.

My sister and I don't like the ghost
that lives in Aunt Dolly's house.
If she was a nice ghost
she wouldn't make the cat hiss
or frighten us when we want to play.
Aunt Dolly speaks of her with fondness,
says she protects her,
stands guard against my uncle —
a veteran —
who is fighting ghosts of his own.

More Than Just Walls

for Kathleen

From my bed under the eaves
I remember the sound of tires on wet morning pavement
after a wild night of thunder and lightning
that finally broke the humidity.
I remember the theme music
of the New Brunswick CBC radio news
every half hour,
a rhythm that takes me back to his kitchen
and being shushed into silence so he could hear the
broadcast.
… a series of sounds that transports me
to a simpler time with a mouth full of white bread,
butter, and molasses.

I remember that winter of mile-high snow drifts
when I went out to clear the dryer vent
and listened to the air puff itself out—
the sound of a modern convenience
that was new for an old house.

I remember my grandfather's smile
as I entered the porch—
my clothes frozen stiff with ice—
and the last time I saw him in his hospital bed.
I showed him my new floppy hat.
He tried it on. It fell over hollow cheeks
and the room filled with his smile.

The memory of my grandfather
rests in wooden baskets filled with berries
in his backyard,
my crimson-stained fingernails traced
the feather limbs of bee-laden asparagus trees.

I say his name—
Walter—
and my mouth fills with the taste
of chalky pink peppermints,
and I hear the snap of the morning porridge fire
rising through the iron grate in the bedroom floor
where, as children, we listened
to nighttime stories of war planes
and Woolworth lunch counters.
Even without people, a house is more than just walls.
His house holds the whisper of ticking clocks, train whistles
and our raspberry-stained laughter.

Tag Sale at Belleisle Creek

A man in mud-caked rubber boots
sits on his porch that sags
like the backside of wash-worn slacks.
He takes a long drag off a home-rolled cigarette,
picks a piece of curled tobacco off his lip.
He slouches down in his chair
stares off to the back field and the hay left to rot.
He was born in this house.

The people who fondle his possessions
hover like crows collecting shiny things.
Price stickers adorn jars, candy tins, spindle-less chairs,
boxes of quilt squares that smell like damp dog,
and a chrome kitchen table that remembers penny pots,
poker chips, and snap peas.

The aroma of aged boards, swollen
with wood smoke and engine oil, wafts
from his garage. In the front yard,
brittle doilies and quilts are draped
over a clothesline—cotton
and lace flap in the breeze.

One quilt remains folded neatly
over his headboard. It smells
of unwashed mornings
and trips to the barn.
On the dresser, droplets
of his wife's toilet water
stain a dresser scarf,
now yellowed and crisp.

My shoes track Upper Canadian dust
into the cracks of pine floorboards
shiny from years of flour and lard.
His kitchen has floral wallpaper
behind a mint green cook stove.
Flypaper from the light fixture,
untwisted, heavy with the weight of flies.

Fingerprints of his long departed
wife remain in the dust on shelves
lined with Mi'kmaq baskets,
woven with tales of tipi summer camps
in the back field, traded for sugar,
mother of pearl buttons, and buckshot.

He sees the world
now through a cloud of cataracts
beneath lids like parchment.
His memory, long atrophied
like the cracked china teacup
he holds in his gnarled hand.
His small musty suitcase is packed
with a few simple items to take to
the single room that awaits him.
He will carry with him things that weigh less
than his sorrow.

In Line with the Past

According to the old folk
there is an art to hanging
clothes on the line —
one load at a time
large items to small
(no undergarments).

On washday each house lays itself bare —

A line of stained dungarees,
coveralls, or bleached white shirts
mean hard work, a man's commitment to family.
The order of the line reveals
a woman's disposition —
how well she cherishes her family
by how she separates colours.
They say the neighbours will compare
whites boiled, bleached,
sun dried.

My whites are grey —
sepia really.
No time for boiling, scrubbing
or beating on rocks.
My line is haphazard,
at best.
Items pinned as they come from the basket —
Red and whites, now pink.

Tale of Forgotten

Tell me the story of the one-lane bridge
past the abandoned mill
and the tea-coloured waterfall.

By the root that grows up through
the pavement leans the house the Loyalists built.
The pasture of someone else's cows
across the way, a fallen cedar fence,
a mound of manure, wasted
on wild mustard and golden rod.

They say an heir burned
the staircase risers and banister for heat,
abandoned the second storey,
ignored the roof that once kept out the rain,
and dismantled the barn to sell off the boards.

They say he used precious photos to light fires
under kindling made from chair rails.
The woodstove once battled draughty windows.
Gales now blow through broken panes.

A grandfather clock with a paralysed
pendulum—seized by neglect—
stands beside a sill thick with dead flies.
Veranda roof wilts above rotting
posts. Broken down eves' trough
sags to the ground.

Tell me the tale of forgotten
silver serving spoons,
of soup ladles and crock pots,
cracked linoleum worn through at the sink,
pounds of potatoes once peeled.

Tell me of quilts, samplers and doilies,
boots of brittle rubber left at the gate,
dog barks lingering at the back screen door
worn past its squeak,
and of hands—now stilled—
that bled at the butter churn.

Tell me of the stillborn, of the ghosts that regret
the toppled gravestones left in the field, and of the
month of Sundays that has finally arrived.

Keirsteadville

I crawl out of bed —
force myself outside to walk,
to placate today's malaise.

I take a neglected path,
to the abandoned house
where forgotten
foundation stones wander
out of place.
Through shattered window glass
I see reflected sun in dark places.
Wild raspberries
scream thorns into shins.

I enter
a one-hinged door.
I imagine dead things on the stoop
left by a clowder of cats.
Inside, failing floors falter,
bare rug ghosts.

My ancestors lived here.
Evenings full of children's laughter,
fiddles and fables
around the dining table.
Pottery shards on pantry shelves,
greasy fingerprints on Formica
are all that is left of those family meals.

Lichened silenced smells
leaves mint-green stains
on timber risers,
nails, hinges, latche —
loose from rusting

Beneath peeled wallpaper
in a bedroom,
sepia stained newspaper
headlining the Spanish Flu
glued to the plaster wall
in a feeble attempt to keep out the cold.

Father

I dreamt I was
in bed with a purring panther
rubbing his furry neck
against my back
as cats do.
As if life was safe in that moment,
surrounded in blackness.

As a child, I climbed
into my parent's bed at night.
My father rubbed my back,
calmed my fears,
reassuring me there is radiance
disguised in darkness
if we are brave enough to look.

Lying beside my father
in each other's arms
in the hospital bed
the day before he died,
our warmth cast light into
the shadow of what was to come.

Warmth, like his stainless steel
teapot on the burner all day;
two tea bags to start,
six by the end of the day—
tea as black as molasses.
As comforting as our last
scotch
in front of the fireplace
that Christmas in Ontario.
Like the smell in my childhood home,
of fermenting wine, baking bread
and the sweetness of Hoya blooms.

Oh, to be born again
with the panthers
or in his garden of lilies,
lying in the pasture under the apple tree
looking at the stars above the Bedford Basin.

Mother Tongue

I

She missed the feeling
of Italian words in her mouth,
the way her tongue continued to vibrate
after she rolled her "r's".
She loved how her inner dialogue
changed language in her head,
how she dreamed in Italian,
and words came to her first in his language.
She missed the misunderstandings they shared
from learning new phrases and unfamiliar words,
the way her mouth got tired late into the evening
from caressing uncommon combinations of vowels.
She missed him, his breathy Florentine accent —
the way his words felt in her mouth.

II

Their journey was long
in distance and years.
How hard it is to learn
a life through strange words —
tired tongues that swallow sounds
as strange as this new land.
They long for their own syllables
to describe their wounds.
Their cultural glances and waving of hands
disobey the new rules they must learn
for an odd way of looking at life.

Their children, too young to remember
how their cheeks felt after a night of Syrian laughter,
now have their mouths stretched full of English.
Arabic sounds will die on a page
that reads from left to right.
Their children's eyes will scan the horizon
in an opposite direction than their ancestors.

III

And what of the language
of this land?
the water of the Bay
that speaks with
the tongue of tides.
a gasp of salt air
cadence of fish and farm
labyrinth of language
sand   soil
veins of aspen
listening
rustle of spruce grouse
against the undergrowth
the alphabet of loam
cradled beneath
constellations
that spell
the words living on
my lips

My Great Aunt and Uncle's Farm

Crayons melt
in the hot summer sun
in the back window of the car.
I cry—
every colour
swirled into a puddle
of molten brown

I am three—
above me a grove
of towering adults
to listen,
to comfort.
My first experience of loss,
and all that colour—gone
behind a blur of tears.
My book full of lines
and me with nothing
to scribble outside them.

A bedroom under the eaves,
slanted roof,
slanted floors—
memories of so much colour.

On the bed, a quilt—
hundreds of fabric pieces
sewed into a patchwork of cozy hues.

Rough floors
ice cold
under my bare feet.
I jump from one bright
hooked rug to another
like a frog on woolly lily pads.

Now,
I stay at home,
watch the days pass —
the landscape is a collage
of windy branches
scratching the sky.
It is overcast,
defused light flattens hue.
I sit beneath our pine,
ponder crayons —
waxy crumbled lines,
grateful
I did not lose myself
forever in that puddle
of brown wax

Anomaly

acidic soil nurtures
lupines in my ditch
their purple petals
rejoice in sharpness
sway in piquant air
impose authority over
other weeds
create beauty
from severity

I am too alkaline
for harshness
accosted by this acrid world
I wilt

I hide from anguish
the burden too great
from severity I emerge broken
not in shades
of pink and purple
reaching

Cougar

*"The cougar before she falls from her high limb
holds for one moment the ponderosa pine, her back
arched, her tail so still the forest stops."*

Patrick Lane
Collected Poems, 2011

You spoke of the cougar
that fell dead from the tree,
the one that left a scar.
I have them too;
bullet filled cougars
within for life,
circling,
reminding me of wounds.

These are the hazards of living
with a poet's heart;
moments that other's
may not have noticed,
let alone carried
within them for life.

The Call

Both your grandmothers heard
unfamiliar voices deep in root cellars,
buried their longings with turnips and pears.

I buried mine in bottles of wine
to quiet the call to a contemplative life.
I know it left a sour taste in your mouth,
my sons,
and the knot in my stomach prevented
you from tying your shoes.

I cursed every potato peel,
choked on the dry turkey and burnt cookies
that declared me a failure.
I almost drowned
in the shallow pool of suburbia —
gagged down small talk.
I know you felt my anger, hid
in the scratchy sleeves of your sweaters.

I painted our living room of winter dogwood.
My silence bled the colour of our walls —
Red was the shade of my longing.

Red Moon

Today, I am silken thread
    on the outside
barbed wire on the inside.
Kindness is not words I say
but the ones I wash down
with bitter tea.

I am glad no one can hear my thoughts—
the ones in cruel crevices of my brain.
I pick scabs of ancient combat wounds,
sew in the lining of my winter coat
the many thoughts I cannot share.

I take my sincere smile
from its hook and tie it onto my face.
On my morning walk
I meet an unfamiliar woman.
She hands me an ornate box.
Inside is her well-rehearsed story—
the small talk of her life,
the bright future of her children,
her renovated kitchen.
As if the box holds jewels
or a tiny ballerina doing pirouettes
to a song I want to hear.
As if I also have a shiny box
that holds my small talk story
instead of the sour stew
that simmers beneath my silence
and the blood that I gargle from biting my tongue.

The Beech Tree

She holds up the kitchen counter, dries the last of the supper dishes, and looks out the window at the twisted limbs of the beech tree she planted when her son was born.

She tastes the bitterness of all that lost time when she could have been writing — when poetry scratched at her eyelids, and she pined for solitude. Years ago, she composed metaphors for spilt milk and shattered tumblers then squirreled them away in her journal — collected words like others collect baby photos. In spring she sat under the beech and longed to be like the robin that taught her babies to fly, then left them to fend for themselves. From an empty nest the robin sang her liberty song and flew to far-off places.

While she read her son *Good Night Moon,* she silently composed poems about celestial bodies. When she read *The Giving Tree* she imagined a place under the beech where she could be alone — a place beneath the weathered bark where she could store her words. In time her musings on resentment would offer nourishment.

After the police brought her son home for egging houses, they both walked on shells. It's hard to write poetry with worry on your words. When she dies, she hopes her son will find a place in the fabric folds of her best dress to hide all the worries and unfinished poems she said she would take to her grave — her son, an artist, now overseas, is unaware of her journals.

With gnarled hands she folds the dishtowel and watches the last of the sunlight flicker through the tree's foliage. In her final years the words fall like leaves, that she rakes into piles and hopes that one day will become the lines of a poem about a mother who sacrificed stanzas for her son.

The Possibility of Amethyst

She used to be a feral child with torn knees
and twigs in her hair.

She had important things to say to those who would listen—
like there are blue spaces that shine through leaves,
that snow isn't really white,
that rosehips contain the promise of spring,
and inside some rocks there are diamonds.

She shouted from the tops of the trees she climbed,
hid in the forts she built, dammed streams she crossed,
and invented names for the colours no one else could see.

When she grew up, she wanted to paint castles in the sky
and write stories about miracles and muskrats that talk.
But as she grew older the feral child began to disappear.

At thirteen, on the shores of Belleisle Bay,
she hated the discomfort of her first Kotex.
She watched the others play in the waves
creating monsters with seaweed hair.
No one told her that women could be wild too.

And when her high school friends
sent her a going away card
at the time the space shuttle embarked
on its voyage,
they laughed and called her a space cadet.
No one told her wanting to soar was a strength.

The night she watched
a documentary on commercial farming,
her friends laughed at her when she wept.
Her heart broke for those cows and pigs
mistreated and murdered, their wildness
cast aside and snuffed out.

Even then, she understood the importance of metaphor.
When her friends spoke, she could hear
the real meaning their words, falling like
black lies obscuring their faces.
She could feel people's pain; she limped
when other's had rocks in their shoes.

Last night, the feral child came in a dream,
Reminding her of that wild, childlike wonder,
And that in rocks in the hearts of grownups
There lies the possibility of amethyst.

Epilogue

Aurora

This dawn prays
itself forward
after a week of rain.

Beyond the river,
verdant hills
in a triad of green.

Gaps between branches
close with layers of foliage
so thick the light bounces

from leaf to leaf,
burnishes bole
with flashes of stars.

The softest of blues
on the new growth of spruce
cradles the scent of loam.

Blossoms of columbine
hold droplets of dew and secrets
of dogwood, parsley, and lace.

Let this summer solstice
not bring a eulogy
for trees. The sharp scent

of spruce seeds the clouds.
Beneath the argil, forests share
the ancient petitions of pine.

Aurora, I cherish your light,
your devotion to dandelions
and your patience for rain.

On this, the truest of mornings,
feral flowers call out
to the wildness of bees.

Notes

A version of "New Brunswick" was first published in *In/Words Magazine*, Vol 15, issue 3.

"Mornings in Erbs Cove" won the 2018 Dawn Watson Memorial Single Poem Prize from the Writer's Federation of New Brunswick.

"*Sol Invictus*" won the 2020 Dawn Watson Memorial Single Poem Prize from the Writer's Federation of New Brunswick.

Acknowledgements

First of all I would like to thank Keith, Brendan and Ellen Helmuth at Chapel Street Editions for their trust in me and this project and for their hard work putting this collection together into a beautiful book.

I would like to thank my editor and mentor Gerard Collins for his hours of work on this manuscript, his patience and guidance.

My deepest gratitude to Beth and Peter Powning. Thanks to Beth for writing the Foreword to this book and to both her and Peter for their friendship and kindness. Also I would like to thank them for all their encouragement for both my writing and my art.

I would like to thank Lorna Crozier and the late Patrick Lane for their patience, wisdom, and expertise at Wintergreen Studios. It was their encouragement that sent me on this journey starting in 2011. I am grateful for Wintergreen Studios. It is sacred space of creativity and stillness in the Frontenac Arch Biosphere Reserve in Ontario. It is where this book was born.

Thank you to my partner David Hansford for the many hours he listened to me read bad poetry, his love and endless encouragement.

To my dear friend Elizabeth Paulette-Coughlin for her insight, encouragement, brilliance, and kindness.

For Denise Connors for her compassion and friendship.

To my friends Magda Lewis and Irene Chisolm for their encouragement and support.

Thank you to Gig Keirstead and Denise Howlett for teaching me so much about the landscape of New Brunswick.

To the Arts and Culture Centre of Sussex for their open mic nights where I read most of these poems for the first time.

To the Writer's Federation of New Brunswick for their support, workshops, contests, and networking opportunities.

To the wonderful people and places of New Brunswick who heal, inspire, and cradle me in the sacredness of this place.

About the Author

Melanie Craig-Hansford graduated from the Nova Scotia College of Art and Design (NSCAD University) in Halifax with a Bachelor of Fine Arts in 1984 and a Bachelor of Art Education in 1985. In 1982 she studied painting in Florence, Italy for a year. Melanie taught High School Visual Art in Alberta and Ontario 1986-2000. In 2000 she took the position of Teacher-Librarian at a high school in Kingston, Ontario where she remained until 2014.

Melanie now lives in Hampton, New Brunswick with her partner David, her son, Sloan, Charlie the cat, and Myles the dog. She dedicates her time to two passions: making art and writing poetry. She has published work in various journals, co-authored a book called *Prayers for Women Who Can't Pray* and more recently had three poems published in a book by Bishop University Press titled *Hope and Resilience in the Time of COVID*.

Melanie has been involved in the Sussex Arts and Culture Centre (AX) for many years. Her work was included in group shows in 2016 and 2022. She has taught workshops and classes in drawing, acrylic painting and watercolour at AX. She has participated in many art festivals, art markets, and had solo shows at the Grand Manan Art Gallery and at the Saint John Art Centre.